Inspire Your Desires
With Cooking

Recipes by: Mother Earth
Illustrations by: Panda Bear Creations

Dedication

I dedicate this book to all of humanity, all of existence. Abounding health and healing of all who are well, and all who suffer. May your path of wellness and self-reflection produce an abundant harvest of Peace and love projected to all. Be joyful, be well in all actions.
-Mother Earth

4

TABLE OF CONTENTS

3. Dedication

9. Be Aware

11. Intro

15. Kitchen Essentials

16. Nut Soaking Times

18. Be Still

19. SNACKS-SAUCES-DIPS-BUTTERS

20. Avocado Mayo

21. Walnut Hempseed Butter

22. Black Sesame Seed Tahini

24. Mixed Bean Hummus

26. Hempseed Pesto

27. Black Sesame Lentil Crackers

28. Wonderful Watercress Sourcream

29. Garlic Ginger Paste

30. Ginger Garlic Sauce

31. Basil Vinegarette

32. Cheese Sauce-Dip

33. Nut Crumble

34. Pumpkin Snack

35. Tasty Turmeric Onion Dip

36. Cilantro Guacamole

37. Ola Seaweed Wraps

38. Cinnamon Pancake Syrup

39. Seasonal Syrup

40. Elderberry Syrup

42. Be Love

43. MEALS - SALADS

44. Easy Lentils

46. Lentil Salad

48. Beet Salad

50. Veggie Sandwich

52. Steamed Brussel Sprouts

53. Steamed Asparagus

54. Asparagus Soup

56. Kale Masala

58. High Vibe Pizza

60. Bitter Melon Tacos – Burritos

62. Creamy Tomato Soup

64. Quinoa tabouli

66. Cauliflower Chili

68. Cream of Mushroom

70. Vegetable Korma

72. Bitter Melon Curry

74. Purple Cabbage

76. Breakfast Potatoes

78. Okra Spaghetti

80. Falafel Burgers

82. Be Powerful

83. DESSERTS

84. Maca-damia Chocolate Frosting

84. Strawberry Cream Frosting

86. Goji Cinnamon applesauce

88. Mango Lime Pie

90. Chocolate Pudding – Chocoalte

92. Crustless Pumpkin Pie

94. Apple Pie

96. Halwa Carrot Dessert

97. Chia Pudding

98. Candied Sweet Potatoes

100. Coconut Crepes

104. Kiwi Goji Jello

106. Spelt Pancakes

108. Be Clear

109. DRINKS

110. Spicy Chocolate Chai

112. Milks

114. Sorrel Punch

115. Kombucha

119. Be Joyful

120. Recommendations

Love is the most important ingredient. —Mother Earth

Be Aware

The food you eat can be either the safest and most powerful form of medicine or the slowest form of poison. –Ann Wigmore

People have a hard time letting go of their suffering. Out of fear of the unknown, they prefer suffering that is familiar. –Thich Nhat Hanh

There are many reasons created around being unable to eat a wholesome regimen. Cost, fear of the unknown and availability. I like to think of food in 2 ways.

1. Insurance policy. The illnesses resulting from harmful habits require health services and treatments that are truly expensive. It's much cheaper to buy fresh, simple foods, and maintain a healthy lifestyle. Consumption and materialism has become priority over what's important. Many organic farms are now delivering to co-ops and directly to homes in an effort to cut costs and be convenient as well.

2. Nourishment. Organic in particular is more nutrient dense, so less is actually more. . It's hard to step out of routine that repetition has found comfort in. Consider this, many of the current habits are destructive and purposed for filling not nourishing ones body. Step out and try something new, whole foods taste great. The flavor can be an adjustment but only because the taste buds have been damaged by foods designed to keep you craving them. They will adjust over a short period of time.
                                                                          – Mother Earth

VIBRATION

Intro

Let's begin this journey with a couple key factors about intentions. I want to introduce easy recipes. Simple as that. I'm looking to help one transition into a healthier lifestyle. Avoiding difficulty, and make cooking easy with ingredients that are easy to acces, is my goal. I have recipes in here that can be added too, twisted, recreated and changed. This is just meant to be a foundation to get started. To jump start creativity. If there's allergies to nuts, try seeds. If it calls for walnuts and all that's available is pecans, use pecans. I purposely avoided some common ingredients to mix it up a bit. Hopefully I can infuse new ideas into any experienced cooks as well. At the end of this book, I will also list sites and contacts that have been helpful to me. Very important factors for me to get across are:

1. Mindful preparation. Mood, intention and emotional state are very important when preparing food. So many studies have shown, energetically, we affect everything. So being positive and putting love into the preparation can be the difference between an ok dish and a phenomenal dish. I have seen and experienced the same meal prepared by the same person on two different occasions, in 2 different moods and they tasted totally different. So being present and putting love into what's being created is so important.

2. Understanding the nourishing factor. Understand on a cellular level, everything put into the body is either feeding the cells what they need to thrive in a healthy way, or not. Being conscious of what's put into the body consistently will initiate

awareness where the communication channels open. So every time something is eaten, there's a reaction from the body that communicates, "Yes!! This is awesome for me", or "no, this is not feeling good at all." Tuning in on a whole new level from what's considered "normal." Through our individuality, also comes variety. Not all foods work well for all people. What works best for an individual can be learned.

3. Feeling good takes on a whole new meaning when having regular bowel movements. Yes I said it, regular bowel movements. Super important!!! Also, knowing nourishment takes place inside and out. The plumbing needs to work right if it's expected for everything else to function properly.

Mind-Body-Soul!! Healthy isn't only what is eaten, so many factors are left out.

Mind! Are you happy? Are you at peace? Or does everything around you feel like chaos? I find that mantras or quotes that inspire are a good constant to incorporate into daily habits. Meditation is amazing and can be started with just putting aside 10 minutes out of the day to spend quiet time with oneself, yes!!! Pay attention to the breath and just tune into the body. Love self and know ones purpose. Say it until it sinks into the psyche and love of self is believed. We are all a creation of God, and we have a dormant power within just waiting for the openness and awareness to discover it. Of course 10 minutes can increase, as it becomes comfortable prioritizing time.

Body! How do you feel physically? This is important because it affects the mind and how one feels about self. This also affects the entire being on an energetic level. A few things that I believe to be a wonderful and sustainable benefit to the body are modalities like yoga, qigong, martial arts, hiking, and rock climbing…. What's of interest? Get outdoors, activate!! Go to a gym if that makes more sense. My point is get moving where the focus is on self. When happy and whole, one is much more equipped to serving.

Soul. Find a path that works. Feel connected, free, and centered. Not guilty, shameful, stressed or fearful. Raise vibration with a healthy spiritual mind. There are beautiful paths, but it is more heartfelt when it's chosen by ones heart.

Mind, body, soul!!! This is not separate. We are a whole, and when we separate these aspects of self, dis-ease can find it's way into our lives. The healthiest food can be consumed, but be a negative, stressed out person and guess what? Sick all the time. This also means speaking ones truth. Being authentic. Speaking truth I have found can be very liberating. We are all different, so our truths will be varied. The world would be less exciting if we were all the same. But all of us create the most beautiful canvas of art and if we don't express fully who we are, that masterpiece is missing an essential part. Find a balance, clear the conditioning that has caused such problems. Begin one step at a time. Don't expect a miracle overnight, although don't reject that idea either. As a wise friend of mine once said, "everything happens in increments" Build upon knowledge. Take everything in stages, and as long as we keep climbing, we get where we want and need to be. Learning to walk includes falling. Language is not learned in a day. Beginning today, we speak, walk and think healthy, whole, and complete. It all begins with the mind, and the only person who creates this reality is self. Love, by caring about every bit of this incredible being within. Lets begin this journey together. I am and always will be on a journey, but I've learned to love it and take all the experiences as learning ones. Times when money was low and I was creating something out of nothing for my family, I still turned up the music and loved whatever came off that stove. Good and bad, all have lessons weaved into them. All emotion is energy in motion. Learning to guide the low vibration, or negative emotions, is a great tool for not only surviving hardship, but maintaining equinimity while enduring hardships. Not always easy, but what is it that a divine being can't handle? Nothing, let's rock!!!

-Mother Earth

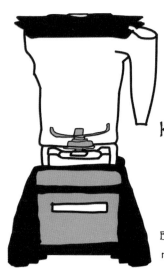

Kitchen Essentials

Blendtec…I will be using a Blendtec Blender for all the recipes that call for blending. Adjustments need to be made if a Blendtec or Vitamix is not available. This is one kitchen appliance worth investing in.

Spiraler…Great for raw pasta and/or salads. Very affordable to buy.

Ice Cream Maker…I use Cuisinart but any brand will do. Get what works or even add ice to the blend to make instant icecream.

Dehydrator…One of my other favorite kitchen appliances! I don't use it much in this book for the sake of keeping things simple and affordable. I prefer the oven types like the Excaliber. Very useful if you're wanting to go deeper into raw food preparation.

Cheese Cloth, Storage Jars, Good Knives… and whatever makes for a pleasant experience in the kitchen.

Nuts Soaking Information

Soaking, draining and rinsing, removes the natural enzyme inhibitors that make it difficult for the body to digest nuts and some seeds. Some don't require soaking like Brazil nuts, macadamia nuts and hemp seeds. General times for the nuts and seeds we use that require soaking:

Walnuts – 2 hours
Pecans – 2 hours
Almonds – 12 hours
Sesame seeds – 4 hours
Flax seeds – 8 hours
Pumpkin seeds – 6 hours

A dehydrator is a very good tool for drying the nuts or seeds after soaking.

The more you extend kindness to yourself, the more it will become your automatic response to others. –Wayne Dyer

INSPIRATION

Be Still and Know That I Am God
Psalms 46:10

Stillness, so simple, but so profound. I find stillness with my
breath. It is and always will be in the present and reminds me to
be aware in the moment. Anytime feelings of tension or stress
arise, take a deep breath, Find stillness. This can be applied in
every aspect of life. Qigong and Tai Chi are amazing modalities
connecting us back to the breath. Meditation around nature,
like rivers and trees, is very grounding. Now how can this be
applied with cooking? Be present, tune in and make that meal a
meditation. Find the joy in nourishing the temple (body), Open
those channels of communication. That food will become one
with the body on a molecular level, make it high vibration.
Love!!!! Now let's cook.
-Mother Earth

If you change the way you look at things, the things you look at change.
—Wayne Dyer

Avocado Mayo

Ingredients: 2 avocados
Pinch of pink salt

Directions: Mash avocado with salt and spread on a sandwich in place of mayo.
Truly simple but so nutritious.

I am free from fear, I am present, I am aware of my divine nature. —Mother Nature

Walnut Hempseed Butter

Ingredients:

1 cup walnuts

1 cup hempseeds

2-3 Tbsp sucanat —optional

½ cup coconut oil melted —less for thicker consistency

Directions:

Pulse in blender 5 seconds, run 1 cycle on speed 10.

Walnut
Hempseed
Butter

It is no coincidence that four of the six letters in health are heal.

—Ed Northstrum

Black Sesame Sesame Seed Tahini

Ingredients:
2 Cups black sesame seeds
1 Cup olive oil
1 cup water
 1/8 tsp. pink salt

Directions: Place all ingredients into the blender, liquids first. Blend 1 cycle on speed 10. This makes a paste, if you want a thinner consistency, add more water until you have your desired consistency.

Keeping your body healthy is an expression of gratitude to the whole cosmos.
−Thich Nhat Hanh

Mixed Bean Zucchini Hummus

Ingredients:
½ cup kidney beans cooked
½ cup chickpeas cooked
1 cup black beans cooked
½ cup diced zucchini
2-3 Tbsp. lemon juice
2 Tbsp. black sesame tahini
2-3 cloves of garlic
2 Tbsp. Olive oil
¼ tsp. pink salt

Directions:
Put all ingredients into the blender. Pulse a few times, then blend 1 cycle on speed 10.

The moment you realize you are enough…live there.
–Stacy Barthe

Hemp Seed Pesto

Ingredients:
2cups packed basil
5cloves garlic
½ cup olive oil
¾ cup hempseeds
½ tsp. pink salt

Directions:
Put all ingredients in blender and pulse for about 10 seconds or until smoothe.

Love, it's a powerful state of being. Be it! – Mother Earth

Black Sesame Lentil Crackers

Ingredients:
½ cup dry brown lentils
1 cup spelt flour
1/8 tsp. black pepper
¼ tsp. garlic powder
1 tsp. pink salt
1 Tbsp. nutritional yeast
1 ¼ cup water
1 Tbsp. flaxseed
1 Tbsp. black sesame seeds
¼ tsp. baking soda
2 tsp. coconut oil melted

Directions:
Powder lentils and flaxseed in blender, by pulsing. Put into a bowl, add the rest of ingredients, mix well. Spread out onto parchment paper, in a think layer. Place on a baking sheet, and cut into squares. Bakes 30-40 minutes at 400 degrees.

Strive that your actions day by day may be beautiful prayers. ~'Abdu'l-Baha

Wonderful Watercress Sourcream

Ingredients:

2 cups watercress chopped

1 cucumber half skin off quartered

2 Tbsp. lemon juice

½ cup coconut oil melted

½ cup almonds or pecans

Directions:

Put all ingredients into blender, liquids first. Pulse a few times, then blend 1 cycle speed 10.

A journey of a thousand miles begins with a single step.
—Confucious

Garlic-Ginger Paste

Ingredients:
25 large cloves of garlic peeled
2 large ginger root pieces peeled
½ cup water

Ginger and garlic should be equivalent in amount.

Directions:
Add all ingredients into the blender and blend 1 cycle at speed 10

If diet is wrong, medicine is of no use. If diet is correct, medicine is of no need.
-Ancient Ayurvedic proverb

Ginger Garlic Sauce

Ingredients:
¼ cup ginger garlic paste
1-2 Tbsp. honey
¼ tsp. black pepper
1 tsp. lemon juice
1 cup olive oil
½ cup apple cider vinegar
½ cup walnuts

Directions: Put all ingredients into blender. Blend 1 cycle at speed 10.

When life knocks you down, roll over and look at the stars. ~Unknown

Basil Vinegarette

Ingredients:
2 packed cups basil
½ cup apple cider vinegar
2 tsp. honey
¼ tsp. black pepper

Directions: Put all ingredients in blender and blend 1 cycle at speed 10.

Food is medicine, and the right kind of relationship with food can make a positive impact on your health. —Hayley Hobson

Cheese Sauce/Dip

Ingredients:

11/3 cup walnuts or pecans - hemp seeds for thinner sauce

2/3 cup water

3 Tbsp. lemon juice

¼ cup nutritional yeast

¼ cup red bell pepper diced

1 tsp. paprika

1 tsp. pink salt

1/8 tsp. cayenne pepper

Directions: Place all ingredients into the blender. Pulse a few times then blend 1 cycle on speed 10. This sauce is great on kale, and bitter melon when you dehydrate them. Also great mixed with chili to make a chili cheese dip. It is a wonderful vegetable dip. A thinner consistency makes it great on nachos.

Whatever you think you can do or believe you can do, begin it. Action has magic, grace and power in it. –Goethe

Nut Crumble

Ingredients:

1 cup macadamia nuts

½ cup pine nuts

3 Tbsp. nutritional yeast

½ tsp. Pink salt

Directions: Put all ingredients into the blender and pulse a few times. Pulse until powdered but not more than that or the oils will make it into a paste. Use a mortar and pestle to finish if needed. Goes great on icecream, goes great on chili.

All that is required to bring peace to the world, ...is for you to shine your light.
—Ray Kamille

Pumpkin Seeds Snack

Ingredients:
Pumpkin
Fine pink salt

Directions:

Scoop seeds out of pumpkin. Separate seeds from pumpkin pulp. Rinse well using a colainder. Using a dehydrator, put the seeds in the unit's tray. Lightly salt if desired. Set the dehydrator to 120 degrees F. Leave the seeds in the dehydrator for about 2-3 hours, or until dried well. If using an oven, lay out on baking sheet and bake at the lowest temperature for 2-3 hours or until dried.

We accept the love we think we deserve.
-Stephen Chbosky

Tasty Turmeric Onion dip

Ingredients:

3" chunk turmeric

¼ cup walnuts

1 avocado

½ cucumber half skin on quartered

1/3 cup water

1 - 1½ tsp. pink salt

¼ cup onion diced

1 clove

1 Tbsp. lemon juice

Directions:

Put all ingredients into the blender and blend 1 cycle speed 10.

There is no drug that can do for you what eating well, moving your body, self love and mindfulness can... ~Bridget Jane

Cilantro Guacamole

Ingredients:
6 avocados
½ cup onions diced
24 sprigs of cilantro finely chopped
1 Tbsp. Lime juice
¾ tsp. pink salt -optional
1 tomato diced
¾ tsp. chili powder

Directions: Peel avocado and put in big bowl, without seed. Add all ingredients and mix well. Avocado will soften on it's own.

To insure good health: eat lightly, breathe deeply, live moderately, cultivate cheerfulness, and maintain an interest in life. —William Londen

Ola Seaweed Wraps

Ingredients:

1 avocado in slcices

2 nori wraps

½ cucumber mooncut

¼ cup hummus

2 Tbsp. beet shredded

1 Tbsp. pumpkin seeds

2 Tbsp. nutritional yeast

½ tsp. pink salt

Directions:

Divide and spread hummus out evenly on each nori wrap in the center. Divide and layer the rest of ingredients on top of hummus. Enjoy.

One should not belittle food-the life breath is food…~Hinduism

Cinnamon Pancake Syrup

Ingredients:
1 cup sucanat
1 cup water
2 tsp. cinnamon
2 tsp. Vanilla bean paste

Directions:
Put all ingredients into the pot. Bring to a boil, reduce heat to a high simmer. Stirring frequently until it starts to thicken. Then remove from heat and let it cool or serve immediately.

You become that which you think you are. Or, it is not that you become it, but that the idea gets very deeply rooted - and that's what all conditioning is. ~Osho

Seasonal Syrup

Ingredients:
2 red onions
Bulb of garlic
Branch of ginger
1 tsp. cayenne pepper - optional
Honey or sucanat

Directions:
Start with some sugar at the bottom of the jar. Layer onion, chopped garlic, chopped ginger, and honey. Repeat making layers all the way to the top of the jar. Seal it tight. Let it sit for 4 hours to 24 hours depending on how strong you want it. Shaking it a couple times a day. Store in a jar and label it.

Serving 1-2 Tbsp 3-4 times a day or less if not needed as much

I am grateful for this day and all that I am. —Mother Earth

Elderberry Syrup

Ingredients:
2 oz. Elderberries
1 tsp. cinnamon
1 pint water
¾ cup honey

Directions:
Bring water to a boil. Put all ingredients except honey in the pot, reduce heat and low simmer covered for 20 minutes. Strain and mix ¾ cup of the tea into ¾ cup honey. Mix well and store in a jar. Label it.
Serving 1-2 Tbsp. In water 3 times a day or less if not needed as much.

There's nothing more beautiful than the way the ocean refuses to stop kissing the shoreline, no matter how many times it's sent away. —Unknown

PURIFY

Be Love

Verily the most necessary thing is contentment under all circumstances...
Yield not to grief and sorrow: they cause the greatest misery. Jealousy
consumeth the body and anger doth burn the liver; Avoid these two as
you would a lion.

-Baha'u'llah

...You should not neglect your health, but consider it the means which
enables you to serve....You should certainly safeguard your nerves, and
force yourself to take time, and not only for prayer and meditation, but
for real rest and relaxation

-Shoghi Effendi

The body in it's amazingness, carries a vibrational frequency. Our
thoughts, emotions, feelings, judgments... the stories we create around
situations and experiences all affect our body on an energetic level. This
is the importance of being present. Reflecting on the world around
oneself and finding peace within. To allow outside circumstance to
control every mood and action, is to be an instrument out of control.
Meditation and like practices allow one to find balance. Learning to
become what we seek. We are powerful instruments. Tune it and play the
melody like it's purposed to play.

~Mother Earth

We don't see things as they are, we see them as we are.
—Anai's Nin

Easy Lentils

Ingredients:

2 cups brown lentils

8 cups water

1 tsp. turmeric

2 tsp. cumin

2 tsp. curry powder

2 Tbsp. garlic ginger paste

2 tsp. coriander

1 tsp. cayenne ~optional

1 ½ tsp. pink salt

Garnish: optional

½ bunch finely cut cilantro

½ onion half moon cut

3-5 garlic cloves minced

1 tsp. whole cumin seeds

¼ cup coconut oil

1 tsp. pink salt

Directions:

Put all ingredients, not including garnish ingredients, into a pot. Bring to a boil. Lower heat, cover and simmer for 40 minutes. Heat onions, garlic cloves, cumin seeds and salt in coconut oil until lightly browned. Stir into pot with fresh cilantro. Serve.

Every movement, every glance, every thought, and every word can be infused with love.—Thich Nhat Hanh

Lentil Salad

Ingredients:

1 ½ cups brown lentils

¼ cup quinoa

1 cucumber diced

¼ cup cilantro cut finely

1 cup balsamic vinegarette

5 cups water

Directions:

Bring water to a boil. Add lentils and quinoa into the pot of water and reduce heat to a simmer. Let cook 20-25 minutes or until cooked. Strain if needed. Put aside to cool. Once cooled, add cucumber, cilantro, and balsamic vinegarette. Mix in well and serve. Other veggies can be added to spruce it up if wanted. Skies the limit with this one.

....and from it (the earth) we produced grain for their sustenance.
Surah 36 Ayat 33

Beet Salad

Ingredients:

3 medium size beets shredded

1 tsp. ginger minced

2 avocados in chunks

1 tomato diced

1 cucumber diced

2 large swiss chard leaves

¼ cup lime juice

2 tsp. mint

1 tsp. pink salt

Directions:

Mix all ingredients well and serve.

Let yourself become living poetry.
—Rumi

Veggie Sandwich

Ingredients:
4 Tbsp. Avocado mayo
Pinch black pepper
1-2 garlic cloves minced
Swiss Chard leaves
Slices of tomato
Zucchini or cucumber slices

Directions:
Apply mayo on both slices of bread, layer the rest of the ingredients. All is optional and many more variations can be used.

Even after all this time, the sun never says to the earth, "you owe me." Look
What happens with a love like that, it lights the whole sky. -Hafiz

Steamed Brussel Sprouts

Ingredients:
1 bag of brussel sprouts
1 tbsp. coconut oil
½ tsp. black pepper
¼ tsp. turmeric
½ tsp. pink salt

Directions:

Put water in a pot and bring to a boil. Put steamer basket in and fill with brussel sprouts. Cover and reduce heat to medium high. Steam 10-15 minutes. Remove from steamer, put brussel sprouts into a bowl and add the rest of the ingredients.

Inhale Love, Exhale Gratitude!

Steamed Asparagus

Ingredients:
1 batch of asparagus
1 tsp. black pepper
½ tsp. pink salt

Directions:

Put water in a pot and bring to a boil. Put steamer basket in and fill with asparagus.
Cover and reduce heat to medium high. Steam 10 minutes. Remove from steamer,
season and serve.

What lies behind us and what lies before us are tiny matters compared to
what lies within us. ~ Ralph Waldo Emerson

Asparagus Soup

Ingredients:

1 pack of fresh asparagus cut into small pieces. (separate the tips)

2 carrots diced

1 onion thinly cut

1 stalk celery diced

5 shitake mushrooms finely cut

2 large cloves of garlic minced

1 tsp. pink salt

2 roma tomatoes diced

¼ cup red bell pepper diced

¼ cup coconut oil

½ cup distilled water

½ cup distilled water

2 Tbsp. olive oil

½ tsp. turmeric

1 tsp. curry powder

Directions: Heat coconut oil on medium high. Add onions and sauté until brown about 10 min. Add seasonings and garlic to ½ cup water and stir. Add to the pan and simmer for 5 minutes. Add everything else except asparagus tips, olive oil and other half cup of water. Simmer 10 minutes stirring often. Let cool about 10 minutes. Add ½ cup water, olive oil, and contents of the pan to the blender leaving about a Tbsp of juice in the pan. Blend for 1 cycle at speed 10. Saute the asparagus tips in the remaining juice in pan for 2 minutes. Add the asparagus tips to the puree and stir them in. Enjoy.

Nothing is impossible, the word itself says 'I'm possible'!"
-Audrey Hepburn

Kale Masala

Ingredients:
1 bunch kale
1 onion thinly sliced
1 cup cooked chickpeas
¼ cup coconut oil
1 tsp. coriander
½ tsp. cumin
½ tsp. mustard powder
1 tsp. chili powder
2 cloves
1 cup water
¼ tsp. garam masala
1 ½ tsp. pink salt
1/8 tsp. cayenne
1 Tbsp. tamarind sauce
¼ cup water

Directions: In a bowl combine ¼ cup water with 1 tbsp tamarind. Mix with your fingers until it creates a sauce mixture. Dispose of the skins and set sauce aside. Heat coconut oil on medium high and saute onions until lightly browned, about 10 minutes. Add all spices together in 1 cup of water and mix well. Add tamarind sauce to your spice mixture. Add to pan with onions. Saute 5 minutes to allow sauce to thicken. Add chickpeas, cook about 10 minutes. Then add kale and cook until the leaves soften, about 10-15 minutes.

A bird doesn't sing because it has an answer, it sings because it has a song."
- Maya Angelou

High Vibe Pizza

Lentil Crust

Ingredients:
1 cup dry lentils any color
¼ tsp. cumin
¼ tsp. garam masala
1 tsp. salt
1 ¼ cup water
2 tbsp. flaxeed
2 tsp. coconut oil
1 Tbsp. coconut oil

Toppings:
½ cup chopped shitake mushrroms
½ cup red/orange bell pepper
1-2 tomatoes diced
½ cup basil leaves chopped
1 Tbsp. nutritional yeast
Cheesy sauce Recipe
Mixed Bean Zucchini Hummus Recipe

Directions:

Powder lentils in blender by pulsing a few times. Then add cumin, garam masala, salt, flax and water into the blender. Blend 1 cycle on speed 10. Mixture should be smoothe like a cake batter. Coat a round or rectangular baking sheet with 1 Tbsp. coconut oil, and pour batter making a thin layer. Using a spatula, spread evenly across the pan. Bake at 350 degrees for 20-30 minutes. It will be a thin crunchy crust. Let it cool to the touch and then spread black bean zucchini hummus covering crust. Cover with cheese sauce and spread vegetable toppings on top. Sprinkle nutritional yeast on top and bake another 10 minutes.

Turn your wounds into wisdom. -Oprah Winfrey

Bitter Melon Tacos/Burritos

Ingredients:

1 bitter melon seeds removed or zucchini diced

1 onion thinly sliced

2 tomatoes diced

¼ of red bell pepper diced

¼ tsp. oregano

1 tsp. pink salt

2 cloves garlic

1/8 tsp. cayenne (optional)

¼ cup coconut oil

¼ tsp. onion powder

½ tsp. turmeric

Toppings:

1 batch watercress sourcream

1 batch cheese sauce

shredded lettuce-spinach-swiss chard

Directions: Soak diced bitter melon in 2 cups water and 1 tsp salt for 30 minutes. Heat up oil on medium high, then add onion. Saute until lightly browned, add seasonings, tomatoes, bitter melon and red bell pepper. Reduce heat to medium, and simmer until vegetables soften, about 10 minutes. Scoop into sprouted taco shells, or tortillas. Put toppings on and serve.

None but ourselves can free our minds. ~Bob Marley

Creamy Tomato Soup

Ingredients:

15 roma tomatoes

1 cup coconut milk

2 Tbsp. spelt flour

4 cloves garlic minced

2 tsp. pink salt

1 tsp. black pepper

1 cup water

¼ cup chopped basil

Directions:

Quarter half the tomatoes and put in blender. Pulse a couple times to blend them but still leave some chunkiness. Pour into a pot. Blend the rest of the tomatoes. Then add to the pot with the rest of the ingredients. Bring to a boil, then reduce heat and simmer for 20 minutes, stirring occasionally.

And, when you want something, all the universe conspires in helping you to achieve it. ~Paulo Coelho

ECSTACY

Quinoa Tabouli

Ingredients:

1 ½ cups quinoa

3 cups water

8 green onions chopped

½ bunch parsley chopped

2 large tomatoes diced

1 large cucumber diced

1 red bellpepper diced

1 orange bellpepper diced

½ cup olive oil

¼ cup lemon juice

2 tsp. pink salt

2 tsp. mint

1 tsp. cumin

½ tsp. black pepper

Directions: Bring water to a boil. Add quinoa, return to a boil. Reduce heat, cover and simmer 15-20 minutes or until fluffy. Set aside to cool. Add lemon juice, olive oil and seasoning and tomato paste together in a separate bowl. Add veggies and cooled quinoa. Mix well and chill.

And the day came when the risk to remain tight in a bud, was more painful than the risk it took to blossom. —Anais Nin

Cauliflower Chili

Ingredients:

1 head of cauliflower cut in small chunks

4 roma tomatoes diced

1 onion thinly sliced

¼ cup coconut oil

¼ red bell pepper diced

1 ½ cup black beans cooked

1 ½ cup red kidney beans cooked

2-3 cloves garlic

1/3 cup water

1 cup water

2 tsp. pink salt

2 Tbsp. chili powder

1/8 -1/4 tsp. cayenne pepper - optional

Directions: On medium high heat, saute onions til lightly browned. Add chili powder, salt, garlic, and cayenne to 1/3 cup water and mix well. Add seasonings to onions. Saute 1 minute, then add bell pepper, tomatoes, 1 cup water, eggplant and all the beans. Bring to a boil, cover, reduce heat to medium low, and simmer 20 minutes.

The secret of change is to focus all of your energy, not on fighting the old, but on building the new. —Socrates

Cream of Mushroom

Ingredients:

2 cup water

2 ½ cups shitake mushrooms cut

1 ½ cups black fungus mushrooms cut

½ onion

3 cloves garlic

1 ½ cups vegetable broth

1/8 tsp. thyme

1-1 ½ tsp. pink salt

¼ tsp. pepper

¼ cup coconut oil

1 cup coconut milk

Directions: On medium high heat, sauté mushrooms, onions, seasonings and garlic in coconut oil for about 10 minutes or until mushrooms soften some. Reduce heat to medium, add vegetable broth and water. Cover and simmer 20 minutes, stirring often. Add milk, simmer another 10 minutes covered. Set aside to cool, then add soup to blender and blend 1 cycle speed 10.

Life isn't about finding yourself. Life is about creating yourself.
-George Bernard Shaw

Vegetable Korma

Ingredients:

1 cup water

½ cup brazil nuts powdered

2 onions thinly cut

3 carrots diced

1 cup peas

1 head cauliflower cut into 1inch size pieces

1 medium size eggplant cubed

½ red bellpepper diced

½ cup coconut oil

1 ½ cups coconut milk

2 Tbsp. ginger garlic paste

1 Tbsp. pink salt

4 tsp. curry powder

2 tsp. turmeric

3 roma tomatoes sauced

1/8 tsp. cayenne

Directions:

Heat pan on medium high with coconut oil. When it's hot, put onions in the oil and saute until browned about 10-15 minutes. Meanwhile,
put all seasonings in 1 cup of water, mix well. Powder the brazil nuts, and sauce the tomatoes with pulsing in the blender. Add seasonings, bellpepper, nuts and tomatoes into the onions. Simmer 10 minutes, stirring occasionally. Sauce will thicken. Add the cauliflower and carrots. Simmer 10 minutes or until vegetables settle and soften a little, stirring occasionally. Add the eggplant, peas and milk. Stir, cover and simmer at medium low for 20 minutes or until eggplant is cooked well, stirring occasionally.

Time saving tips: cut and have all veggies separated before starting and seasoning in water and ready to go.

Food for the body is not enough. There must be food for the soul. –Dorothy Day

Bitter Melon Curry

Ingredients:

½ cup coconut oil

1 large onion cut into thin slices

½ cup brazil nuts powdered

1 medium size bitter melon seeds removed diced

1 sweet potato diced

3 zucchini cut thin into moon slices

1 large celery stalk diced

4 roma tomoatoes diced

½ cup red lentil

1 cup water

¼ to ½ tsp. cayenne - optional

1 Tbsp. pink salt

2 Tbsp. ginger/garlic paste

1 tsp. turmeric

2 tsp. cumin

2 tsp. curry

4 tsp. coriander

Directions:

Soak bitter melon in a bowl with 2 cups of water and 1 tsp. salt for 30 minutes. Heat ½ cup coconut oil in a deep skillet at medium high heat. When oil is hot, add onions, and sauté for 10 minutes or until onions have browned. Add seasonings to 1 cup of water and stir well. Then add that water to the browned onions. Simmer 5 minutes. Next, add diced tomatoes and powdered brazil nuts, simmer 2 minutes. Then add all vegetables, simmer 5 minutes while stirring. Add lentils and 1 cup water, stir. Reduce heat to medium low, cover and simmer for 20 minutes. Stirring every 5 minutes or so.

Be yourself, everyone else is already taken. -Oscar Wilde

Purple Cabbage

Ingredients:
1 head of cabbage shredded
½ cup coconut oil
2 cloves garlic
1 tsp. cumin
1 tsp. turmeric
1 tsp.pink salt
½ tsp. black pepper
2 carrots finely chopped
¼ cup water

Directions: Warm oil, add all ingredients, mixing well. Bring to a simmer and cook for 15 minutes.

If you think you are too small to make a difference, try sleeping with a mosquito.
— Dalai Lama XIV

GRATITUDE

Breakfast potatoes

Ingredients:

3 medium size purple sweet potatoes or sweet potatoes diced

1 medium size red onion

¼ head of purple cabbage

2 carrots diced

½ red bell pepper

1/4 cup coconut oil

1 cup water

2 tsp. pink salt adjust if needed

1 tsp. turmeric

½ bitter melon seeds removed and diced -optional

Directions: Heat oil on medium high. Lightly brown onions, add potatoes, and carrots. Stir until well coated with oil. Add salt and turmeric. Add bell pepper, and cabbage. Mix well, reduce heat to a simmer and cover. In about 5 minutes, add water, stir and cover again for about 15 minutes, stirring occassionally.

I must be willing to give up what I am in order to become what I will be.
— Albert Einstein

Okra Spaghetti

Ingredients:
1 onion thinly sliced
½ cup coconut oil
1 cup okra diced
½ cup water
2 roma tomatoes diced
1 zucchini diced
1 head broccoli cut into small florets
1 tsp. turmeric
2 tsp. cumin
2 tsp. curry
4 tsp. coriander
1 Tbsp. pink salt
¼ tsp. cayenne powder

Noodles: Large mixing bowl
2 zucchinis spiraled or bag spaghetti noodles
½ cup olive oil
¼ tsp. black pepper
2 large cloves garlic minced

Directions: Sauté onions on high heat in coconut oil until brown, about 10 minutes. Put seasonings into half cup of water, mix well. Pour into pan with onions, add tomatoes and sauté 5 minutes to thicken sauce. Add zucchini, broccoli and okra. Reduce heat to medium, cover and simmer for about 20 minutes, stirring often. Meanwhile, in large mixing bowl add spiraled zucchini or cooked noodles into the bowl. Add olive oil, black pepper and garlic. Toss well. When Sauce with vegetables finishes, add over noodles and serve.

There are only two ways to live your life. One is as though nothing is a miracle. The other is as though everything is a miracle. -Albert Einstein

Falafel Burger

Ingredients:
2 cups chickpeas cooked
1 small onion chopped fine
1 Tbsp. cilantro cut fine
3 cloves garlic minced
1 Tbsp. parsely cut fine
4 Tbsp. spelt flour
1 tsp. salt
1 tsp. cumin
1 tsp. coriander
2 tsp. baking powder
1 Tbsp. water
1 Tbsp. coconut oil

Directions: Dissolve baking powder in water. Mix all ingredients together mashing the chickpeas. Pulsing in the blender or using a food processor will give a finer consistency. Form patties, brush with coconut oil, and place on a baking sheet. Bake at 350 degrees for 20-30 minutes.

Forgiveness is the fragrance that the violet sheds on the heel that has crushed it.
—Mark Twain

Be Powerful

By choosing your thoughts, and by selecting which emotional currents you release and which you will reinforce, you determine the quality of your light. You determine the effects that you will have on others, and the nature of the experiences of your life.
-Gary Zukav

Just feel the magic in the air and the power in the breeze, feel the energy of the plants, the bushes and the trees, let yourself be surrounded by nature at its best, calm yourself, focus and let magic do the rest. ~Sally Walker

I love this as a reminder that we choose. We're in control. Many times we feel victim to our bodies, our surroundings, our habits, our thoughts, our stories, our friends, our jobs…. Perspective can align these creations. Where is the focus? Close your eyes, feel the magic!! Take a deep breathe!! Take another one!! How incredible you are, divine creation!! Everything around you is grand, is sacred. Watch the stars at night and remember the beauty. Everyone has purpose! The mere fact of being in existence means purpose. Create circumstance! Focus determines direction. Begin within. Love self! Love others! Experience the oneness. Believe so deeply, that desires and dreams have no choice but to step into reality.
~Mother Earth

Everything Changes when you start to emit your own frequency rather than absorbing the frequencies around you. When you start imprinting your intent on the universe rather than receiving an imprint from existence. ~ Barbara Marciniak

DESSERTS

Born to give joy and bring peace to the world. —Fo-pen-hing-tsih-king

Maca – damia Chocolate Frosting

Ingredients:

2 cups macadamia nuts

1 cup maple syrup grade b

1 Tbsp. Vanilla bean paste

¼ cup coconut oil

1 tsp. maca root

Directions: Add all ingredients to blender, blend 1 cycle speed 10.

Strawberry Cream Frosting

Ingredients:

6 oz. Coconut yogurt

4 strawberries

½ cup sucanat powdered

1 tsp vanilla bean paste

1 cup pecans or almonds

Directions: Put sucanat in blender, pulse until it's powdered 5-10 seconds. Add the rest of the ingredients into blender. Blend 1 cycle on speed 10.

Respond to every call that excites your spirit. —Rumi

Goji Cinnamon Applesauce

Ingredients:

8 gala apples quartered

¼ cup goji berries (or honey to desired sweetness)

1-2 Tbsp. cinnamon

2 cups water

Directions:

Add all ingredients into a pot, cover and boil at medium high for 10 minutes or until apples soften. Stirring occasionally. Watch to make sure it doesn't boil over. Remove from heat and let cool for 10-15 minutes. Cool longer if desired. Add all contents from the pot into blender and blend at speed 10 for 1 cycle.

Loves greatest gift is its ability to make everything it touches sacred. –Rumi

REFLECTION

Mango Lime Pie

Ingredients:

Crust:

1 cup almonds

½ cup black walnuts

¼ cup coconut flour

2 cups dates

Filling:

3 mangos without seed

½ cup maple syrup Grade B

½ cup lime juice

1 cup coconut oil, melted

Directions:

Crust ~ Add nuts, coconut flour and dates to blender, in that order. Hold down pulse until dates mix in and blender stops blending smoothly, about 5-10 seconds. Take out of blender and hand knead into a ball until consistency is like dough. Press into a pie plate starting from the center working your way to the edges, until evenly spread throughout pan. You can use a fork to give it a pie crust look by pressing with the fork flat around the edges. Optional, for a firmer crust, dehydrate crust for 2 hours at 110 degrees.

Filling - Add lime juice, maple syrup, coconut oil and mangos into the blender in that order. Pulse a few times to get it started and then blend 1 cycle on speed 10. Pour into the pie plate and chill for 2-3 hours.

Nothing is more attractive than being your authentic self. ~Dawn Gluskin

Chocolate Pudding-Chocolate Pie

Ingredients:

2 avocados

½ cup maple syrup grade B

½ cup raw cacao powder

¼ cup coconut milk

Directions:

Put maple syrup, coconut milk, raw cacao powder and avocados in the blender, in that order. Pulse a couple times, then blend for 1 cycle at speed 10. This can easily be turned into a pie by adding ¾ cup coconut oil. Pour it into prepared crust and chill in the refridgerator 2-3 hours or until firm.

We are here to awaken from the illusion of separateness. –Thich Nhat Hanh

SOULFUL

Crustless Pumpkin Pie

Ingredients:

¼ cup water

1 cup coconut milk

1 Tbsp. agar agar powder

2 cups pumpkin puree (1 can 15oz.)

1 cup sucanat

2tsp. cinnamon

½ tsp. ginger powder

¼ tsp. nutmeg

¼ tsp. clove powder

1 tsp. vanilla bean paste

Directions:

Dissolve agar agar in the water on medium heat. Add coconut milk, and pumpkin puree, stir often on a simmer. Stir until pumpkin is liquefied, about 5-10 minutes. Turn heat off, add sucanat, cinnamon, ginger, nutmeg,cloves and vanilla. Mix well. Pour into a pie plate. Chill 1-2 hours. This pie can be warmed, but for a very short period. If using a crust, pre bake the crust before putting the filling in.

Be guided by spirit and not driven by ego. —Unknown

Apple Pie

Ingredients:

3-4 large apples

4 Tbsp. water or tea

½ cup sucanat

3 Tbsp. solid coconut oil

1 Tbsp. apple pie spice

1 tsp. cinnamon

1 Tbsp. spelt flour

Directions:

Line pie plate with crust. Cut each apple into 8 pieces, removing the core first. Make even layer into prepared dish. Add water. Cut pieces of coconut oil and disperse over the apples. Sprinkle with sucanat, pie spice, cinnamon and spelt flour. Put top crust over the top. Cutting into strips and overlapping is also a great option. Cut 4 slits into crust and use a fork to make the ridges along the edge. Use foil on the edges to prevent burning while baking.

With every breath, I honor the Divine and live in gratitude.
—Eva Trinity

Halwa Carrot dessert

Ingredients:

3 cups Milk

4 cups carrots shredded

¼ cup coconut oil

1 tsp. turmeric

1 Tbsp. cardamom

1 cup sugar

1 Tbsp water

Directions:

Saute carrots in coconut oil 5 minutes. Add milk, bring to a boil. Lower heat to a good simmer. Simmer 25 minutes or until carrots absorb all the milk. Stir often. Add sucanat. Dissolve turmeric and cardamom in water, add and mix well. Chill

If you can not pronounce it, don't eat it. –Common Sense

Chia Pudding

Ingredients:
1 cup chia powder
¼ tsp. salt
½ tsp. cinnamon
3 Tbsp. sucanat
½ cup applesauce
1 ¾ cup coconut milk

Directions: This dish can be eaten raw, just mix ingredients and let sit for 5-10 minutes to thicken. Also can be heated for about 10 minutes or until thickens for a warm pudding.

A ship is safe in harbor, but that's not what ships are for. ~William G.T. Shedd

Candied Sweet Potatoes

Ingredients:

4 sweet potatoes quartered

5 cups water

1 cup coconut milk

1 tsp. cinnamon

½ tsp. allspice

2 Tbsp. honey

Directions: Fill Pot with water, and potato chunks. Bring to a boil. Boil until fork goes into potato without effort. About 30-40 minutes. Strain water off, add potatoes to a large mixing bowl. Add coconut milk, cinnamon, allspice, honey and mix well. Mixing with a spoon can retain some chunky texture, using a hand mixer will give you a really smooth texture.

All the darkness in the world cannot extinguish the light from a single candle.
—St. Francis of Assisi

Coconut Crepes

Ingredients:

Coconut flesh from 3 young Thai coconuts

¼ tsp. cinnamon

½ Cup coconut water (or water)

Directions:

Blend all ingredients together for 1 cycle speed 10. Pour onto non-stick dehydrator sheets creating circles or squares. Dehydrate at 110 degrees for about 6-8 hours. Until dry but still pliable.

Cream

Ingredients:

½ cup walnuts

1 ½ cup pecans

½ cup coconut water (or water)

¼ cup maple syrup

1 tsp. vanilla

Directions: Place all ingredients into blender liquids first, and blend for 1 cycle at speed 10. It will be thick. Chill for 1 hour

Fruit Sauce

¼ cup goji berries
½ cup blueberries (or fruit of choice)
2 tsp. maple syrup
¼ cup water

Directions: Place all ingredients into blender and blend for 1 cycle at speed 10.

Putting it all together

Directions: Scoop cream into the center of the coconut wrap and drizzle a little sauce over it. Roll it up and when finished with all of them. Drizzle the remaining sauce over the crepes.

Simplicity
Patience
Compassion
~Lao Tsu

DREAM

Kiwi Gogi Jello

Ingredients:
6 kiwis peeled
½ cup goji berries
2 kiwis cut in chunks
4 tsp. agar agar powder
2 cups water
1-3 Tbsp. honey

Directions:
Boil 1 cup of water. Add agar and stir until completely dissolved. May take a couple minutes. Meanwhile, blend kiwis and gojis with honey in the blender. Add 1 cup of water to the pot and contents from blender. Mix well and pour into molds or dish. Add chunks of kiwi into the jello mixture. Chill for about an hour.

It helps to remember that everyone is doing their best from their level of conciousness. —Deepak Chopra

Spelt Pancakes

Ingredients:
1 ¼ cup spelt flour
1 Tbsp. Sucanat
2 tsp. baking powder
1 ¼ cup coconut milk or water
¼ tsp. vanilla bean paste
1 Tbsp. Coconut oil
Coconut oil for the pan

Directions:
Add dry ingredients into a mixing bowl. Stir well. Make a hole in the center of the bowl, add wet ingredients. Milk should be room temperature to prevent the oil from hardening. Mix leaving the batter a little lumpy. Heat skillet to low medium heat. Coat pan with coconut oil. Pour batter into the pan the size you want your pancake to be. Watch for bubbling on the top, that's when it's time to flip the pancake. Repeat for every pancake. Serve with Cinnamon Syrup and your favorite berries.

I have greater trust of what is true inside of me than what seems to be true outside of me. —John Morton

Be Clear

By cleansing your body on a regular basis and eliminating as many toxins as possible from your environment, your body can begin to heal itself, prevent disease, and become stronger and more resilient than you ever dreamed possible!
~Dr. Edward Group III

To keep the body in good health is a duty, for otherwise we shall not be able to trim the lamp of wisdom, and keep our mind strong and clear. Water surrounds the lotus flower, but does not wet its petals. ~Buddha

To feel good, and be clear is such a gift. It takes effort, but effort is worth the rewards. Our bodies are capable of pushing through the most amazing things, but if we aren't feeding our systems on a cellular level that which it requires and understands, then dis-ease is being welcomed with the red carpet rolled out. . What's the point of having all the money in the world, without the wherewithal to enjoy it or be able to help others? The intention here is to infuse the wonder and clarity of vision. Don't allow the influx of information to be overwhelming. Keep it simple, keep it fresh! If you can't read it, don't eat it. Bring joy into exploration and enjoy the process of learning if going deeper is desired adventure.

.

~Mother Earth

If you stumble, make it part of the dance. ~Unknown

Spicy Chocolate Chai

Ingredients:

4 cups coconut milk

2" chunk of ginger

1 tsp. maca root powder

2 tsp. cinnamon

½ tsp. cardamom

4 cloves

2-4 Tbsp. honey

¼ cup goji berries

1 tsp. vanilla bean paste

¼ cup raw cacao

Descriptions: Put all ingredients in the blender and run 1-2 cycles at speed 10 depending on whether you want it warm or hot.

...each whisper of life and breath has maximation of thankyou..
-Memnon Teze Zaahir

Milks

Almond Milk
Ingredients:
1 cup nuts - almonds, pecans, or walnuts
4-6 cups water
sweeten if desired

Hemp Milk
Ingredients:
2 cups hempseeds
4-6 cups water
Sweeten if desired

Directions:
Blend 1 cycle speed 10. Using a cheesecloth or nut milk bag, strain if desired. The powder can be dehydrated and used as a flour.

Knowing others is wisdom, knowing yourself is enlightenment. –Lao Tzu

REFRESH

Sorrel Punch

Ingredients:
2cups dry sorrel
8 cups water
1 cup sucanat
2 cinnamon sticks
4 cloves
¼ cup minced ginger

Directions:
Bring water to a boil. Add Sorrel, cinnamon, ginger and cloves. Stir and reduce heat to a simmer. Simmer 10 minutes. Add sucanat, stir til dissolved. Strain and chill.

I smile like a flower, not only with my lips, but with my whole being.
~Rumi

Kombucha

Ingredients:

3-5 bags of green or black tea

1 cup sugar

1 gallon water

1 scoby

2 cups starter tea

Supplies Needed:

1 gallon glass jar

1 paper towel or cheescloth

1 rubber band

Directions: Clean all materials and wash hands well before starting. Boil 4 cups water. Turn off heat and steep tea for 8-15 minutes depending on the tea. Remove tea bags, add sugar. Stir until dissolved completely. Pour into gallon jar. Add the rest of the water leaving room for the 2 cups of starter tea and the scoby. When it feels room temperature and is no longer hot, add the scoby and starter tea. Add more water if needed to fill jar. Cover with cheesecloth and bind down with a rubber band. The scoby then does the rest. Depending on the temperature in your house, it can take anywhere from 7 days to 2 weeks. Send positive energy daily and place the jar in a peaceful area. I've never had mold when making kombucha, and I truly believe it's for this reason. Watch for mold, the appearance is similar to what you'd see on bread or food going bad.

Labeling helps to remember when you started it. You might notice a thin layer growing over your mushroom. This is the baby that you can share with others or use for more batches. The mother is reusbale as well. Now when you are ready to test your kombucha to see if it's ready. Stick a straw in and taste it. If it's sour, bottle immediately and reduce the days next time around. If really sweet, let brew a few more days. You are looking for a sharp acidic taste, not sweet. When it's ready, put scoby in a jar with 2 cups tea. Enjoy the rest or flavor it with your favorite taste. I flavored this one with a puree of strawberries and cherries. For the strong evervescence found in store bought kombucha, You can cap it off tightly for 2 more days of brewing. At least twice a day let air into it to prevent it from exploding. Enjoy

The heart surrenders everything to the moment. The mind judges and holds back.
                                        —Ram Dass

BLOSSOM

Be Joyful

Your body makes new cells from the food you eat. What you eat literally becomes you.
You are what you eat.
I love food and I'm an advocate of eating foods that are free from harmful chemicals and nourishing by nature. I know that foods alone do not constitute good health. Thoughts, environment, and activity all play a part in whole-being. It's not about longevity, it's about quality of life. Love of self shows it's presence in how one cares for themselves. Create moments to nourish the physical, practices that keep the body efficient and flexible. Passion, and love is a beautiful guide for the body and mind. Everyone is unique. One of my favorite things to do is dance and sing while I'm cooking, moving with a smile. Love life from within, take pleasure in nourishment, and reflect that beauty back out into the world.
~Mother Earth

I'm going to make everything around me more beautiful...that will be my life.
~Elise de Wolfe

Recommendations

Natural Skin Care....................www.btyliskintherapies.com

Superfoods, tonics, herbs...... www.foodhealing.org

Food Healing Info.....................www.conqueringanydisease.com

Herbs...www.mountainroseherbs.com

Orgone Pyramids.......................www.iammagick.com

Kombucha Kits..........................trishalgoodridge@gmail.com

Blendtec....................................www.motherearthis.com

To attain radiant health, one must fuel the body with the highest quality foods and herbs, while cultivating inner peace through meditation, energy practices, and laughter. –Michael Bouvier

I want to thank everyone who's inspired me and has been a crucial part of my growth. Specificly Wahida Khan, Ola Sobanski, Lisa Washington, Trisha Goodridge and Shellie White Light for the lessons, advice, amazing feedback and creative inspiration during this process. To my family Machai, Valance, Vashon, and Javad for support and being my tasters. Panda Bear for keeping it fun and being such a beautiful spirit.
–Mother Earth

Collaborative effort by Mother Earth and Panda Bear Creations. Thank you for your purchase and many blessings on your path in life. This is a dream of ours to do a book together and so much love and effort went into it's creation. May you find value and lots of fun in it's usage. Love, Ase and Namaste!!!
–Mother Earth and Panda Bear

For more information, please visit us at www.motherearthis.com and www.pandabearcreations.com

As nature, whatever and whoever I need in this day will come to me. I have more than enough. I am never in need. So I rest my worries and all my concerns with God.
—Lisa Washington

7683946R00067

Made in the USA
San Bernardino, CA
13 January 2014